Horrid Henry's
Annual 2012

Horrid Henry's Annual 2012

Francesca Simon

Illustrated by Tony Ross

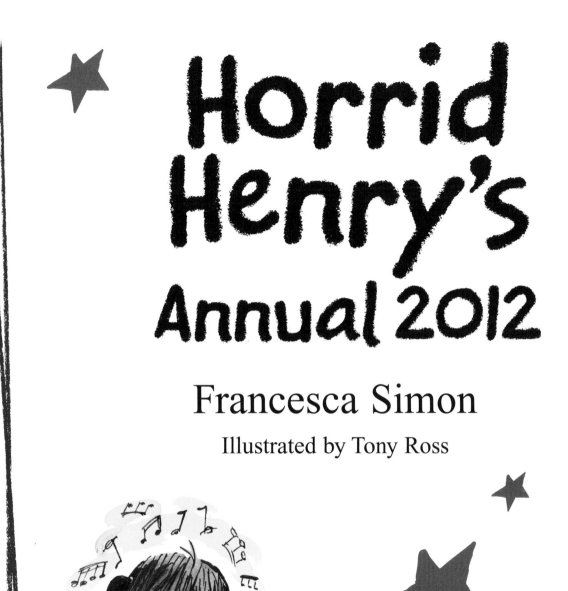

Orion
Children's Books

First published in Great Britain in 2011
by Orion Children's Books
a division of the Orion Publishing Group Ltd
Orion House
5 Upper Saint Martin's Lane
London WC2H 9EA
An Hachette UK Company

1 3 5 7 9 8 6 4 2

This compilation, *Horrid Henry's Annual 2012* © Orion Children's Books 2011
Design by Envy Design Ltd
Text © Francesca Simon 2011
Illustrations © Tony Ross 2011

Compiled by Sally Byford from the *Horrid Henry* books
by Francesca Simon & illustrated by Tony Ross

The Orion Publishing Group's policy is to use papers that are natural, renewable and recyclable
products and made from wood grown in sustainable forests. The logging and manufacturing processes
are expected to conform to the environmental regulations of the country of origin.

A catalogue record for this book is available from the British Library.

Printed and bound in Italy

ISBN 978 1 4440 0168 6

www.orionbooks.co.uk
www.horridhenry.co.uk

Contents

Hello Fans,

Yo, rock fans! Welcome!

It is I, the biggest, baddest, rock superstar in the universe. Yeah! Who was the special guest star with the Killer Boy Rats? Who sang "Gonna be a rock star (and you ain't)" live on stage? (Okay, so it was at the horrible Daffy and her Dancing Daisies concert, but it got me backstage at the Killers.) And who got two free Killer Boy Rats tickets? Me, Me and Me!

Let's make 2012 the screamiest, stompiest year yet. Shout out all the utterly wicked, totally brilliant lyrics sent in by YOU, and discover who makes it to Christmas number one.

Rock out, everyone!

Henry

How Many Rock Guitars?
How many rock guitars can you find hidden in the Annual? Here's the first one.

Henry's Rock Star New Year's Resolutions

 Become the most famous rock star in the world.

 Become the richest rock star in the world.

3 Everyone must bow whenever I walk into a room.

4 No more school: who needs to spell when you're a rock star?

5 Tons more pocket money – how can I afford all my new drum kit on 50p a week???

6 No more homework – I'm far too busy writing brilliant songs like "I'm in my coffin/ No time for coughin'".

Do De Doo De Doooo

7 Peter will give up his bedroom for all my guitars and drums and go sleep in the shed.

LYRICS COMPETITION

When Horrid Henry's favourite band, The Killer Boy Rats, needed a new song, Purple Hand Gang members everywhere sent in lyrics in their thousands.

Francesca Simon chose a winner and five runners-up – you can find their brilliant lyrics throughout the Annual. Enjoy!

Horrid Henry's Rock Star Car

Horrid Henry doesn't want a boring family car like Mum and Dad's. He wants a top-of-the-range, super-deluxe model with all the latest gadgets and gizmos, specially designed for his rock star lifestyle.

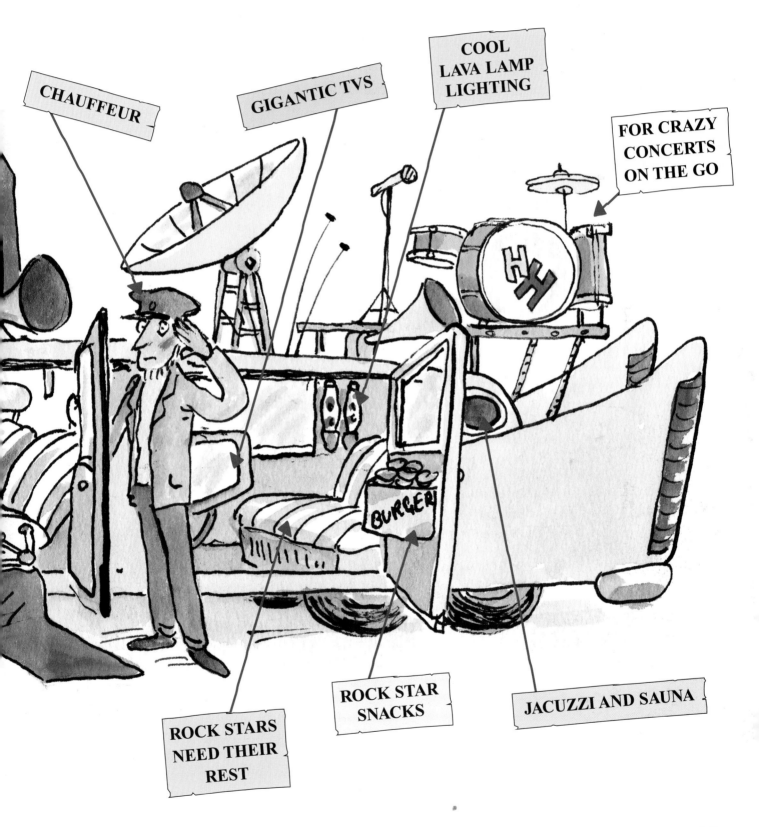

CHAUFFEUR

GIGANTIC TVS

COOL
LAVA LAMP
LIGHTING

FOR CRAZY
CONCERTS
ON THE GO

ROCK STARS
NEED THEIR
REST

ROCK STAR
SNACKS

JACUZZI AND SAUNA

Horrid Henry Rocks

AAAAARRRRRGGGGGHHHHHH.

Moody Margaret's parents were taking her to the Killer Boy Rats concert. Rude Ralph was going to the Killer Boy Rats concert. Even Anxious Andrew was going, and he didn't even like them. Stuck-Up Steve had been bragging for months that he was going and would be sitting in a special box. It was so unfair.

No one was a bigger Rats fan than Horrid Henry. Henry had all their albums: Killer Boy Rats Attack-Tack-Tack, Killer Boy Rats Splat! Killer Boy Rats Manic Panic.

"It's not fair!" screamed Horrid Henry. "I want to see the Killers!!!!"

"We have to see something that everyone in the family will like," said Mum. "Peter's too young for the Killer Boy Rats but we can all enjoy Daffy."

"Not me!" screamed Henry.

Oh, why did he have such a stupid nappy baby for a brother? Younger brothers should be banned. They just wrecked everything. When he was King Henry the Horrible, all younger brothers would be arrested and dumped in a volcano.

In fact, why wait?

Horrid Henry pounced. He was a fiery god scooping up a human sacrifice and hurling him into the volcano's molten depths.

"AAAIIIIIEEEEEEE!" screamed Perfect Peter. "Henry attacked me."

"Stop being horrid, Henry!" shouted Mum. "Leave your brother alone."

"I won't go to Daffy," yelled Henry. "And you can't make me."

"Go to your room," said Dad.

Find out what happens in '**Horrid Henry Rocks**' from **Horrid Henry Rocks**.

New Year's Eve Word Search

Horrid Henry plans to party like a rock star on New Year's Eve, but his parents send him to bed early. Find all the things Henry *should* be enjoying in the puzzle below.

PARTY   BALLOONS
FUN   COUNTDOWN
NOISE   FIZZYWIZZ
MUSIC   CRISPS
MIDNIGHT   DANCING

N	O	I	S	E	Y	E	E	T	E
G	W	O	C	E	G	R	N	U	F
S	N	O	O	L	L	A	B	W	I
P	M	I	D	N	I	G	H	T	Z
S	A	N	C	T	T	S	J	K	Z
I	H	R	Y	N	N	J	M	M	Y
R	A	X	T	F	A	U	I	S	W
C	N	P	H	Y	S	D	O	O	I
A	A	Q	Z	I	L	A	F	C	Z
Y	W	D	C	X	Z	T	X	T	Z

Brainy Brian's Noisy New Year Quiz

1. **What is Horrid Henry's favourite kind of music?**

   (a) Loud and shouty
   (b) Pretty and tuneful
   (c) Soft and slow

2. **When Horrid Henry and his family are in the car Horrid Henry wants to listen to the Driller Cannibals' Greatest Hits. What tape would Perfect Peter like?**

   (a) None – he'd like silence
   (b) A story tape
   (c) The Killer Boy Rats

3. **Who plays the piano at Miss Impatience Tutu's Dance Studio?**

   (a) Miss Basher
   (b) Miss Cracker
   (c) Miss Thumper

4. **What kind of music does Horrid Henry's dad like?**

   (a) Classical
   (b) Country and Western
   (c) Heavy rock

5. **When Moody Margaret stays at Horrid Henry's house, how does she wake everyone up in the morning?**

   (a) By screaming
   (b) By playing her trumpet
   (c) By knocking loudly on the bedroom doors

6. What is the correct name of one of Horrid Henry's favourite bands?

(a) Hairy Hellhound

(b) Horrible Hellhound

(c) Happy Hellhound

8. When Horrid Henry stays at Great-Aunt Ruby's, what scares him in the night?

(a) Stuck-up Steve creeping into the room with a Goo-Shooter

(b) A ghostly breathy moaning sound

(c) Great-Aunt Ruby singing in the shower

7. Which character is best known for her loud screams?

(a) Miss Battle-Axe

(b) Singing Soraya

(c) Moody Margaret

How did you do? Turn to page 74 to find out. Score one point for each correct answer.

6 – 8

HOORAY! You're ready to rock into the New Year with a GREAT BIG NOISY BANG!

3 – 5

You're singing the right tune, but it's time to turn up the volume and try again!

1 – 2

Shhhh. A score like this needs to be kept very quiet.

King Henry the Horrible's Time Line

HOORAY! I'm born and crowned King Henry the Horrible.

I'm elected Lord High Excellent Majesty of the Purple Hand Gang.

I lose my first royal tooth.

All the dinosaurs die a horrible death

I'm forced to have an injection. But kings don't need them!

Poopy pants Peter loses his first tooth – before the King. It's not fair!

THE WORST DAY EVER. Nappy face Peter is born.

The Purple Hand Gang raid Moody Margaret's Secret Club. VICTORY!

I defeat loads of my worst enemies with cunning plans – Stuck-up Steve, the Demon Dinner Lady and Rabid Rebecca the Bogey Babysitter. Nah nah ne nah nah!

I win the WORST prize ever at the School Fair.

TO MY FUTURE
⟶

I beat everyone at Gotcha. Kings can make up their own rules.

The Secret Club stinkbombs the Purple Hand fort.

Pancake Day Puzzle

Between them, Horrid Henry, Perfect Peter and Greedy Graham eat 15 pancakes. Using the clues, can you work out how many pancakes each of them ate and which were their favourite fillings?

FAVOURITE FILLINGS: Lemon juice, jam, chocolate sauce

	NUMBER OF PANCAKES	FAVOURITE FILLING
HORRID HENRY	5	~~chocolate sauce~~ Jam
PERFECT PETER	2	Lemon Juice
GREEDY GRAHAM	8	chocolate sauce

CLUES

1. Greedy Graham ate the most pancakes. He ate 8, but he didn't eat them with chocolate sauce.

2. Horrid Henry ate 3 more pancakes than Perfect Peter.

3. Perfect Peter covered his pancakes with lemon juice.

Are You an April Fools' Day Fool?

Horrid Henry loves playing tricks on April Fools' Day.
Do you love it too, or are you the one who always gets fooled?

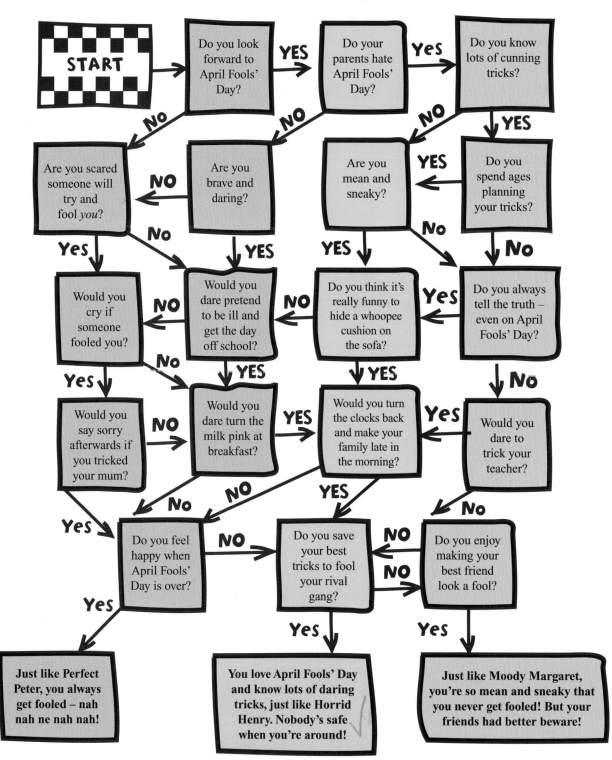

START

Do you look forward to April Fools' Day?

Do your parents hate April Fools' Day?

Do you know lots of cunning tricks?

Are you scared someone will try and fool *you*?

Are you brave and daring?

Are you mean and sneaky?

Do you spend ages planning your tricks?

Would you cry if someone fooled you?

Would you dare pretend to be ill and get the day off school?

Do you think it's really funny to hide a whoopee cushion on the sofa?

Do you always tell the truth – even on April Fools' Day?

Would you say sorry afterwards if you tricked your mum?

Would you dare turn the milk pink at breakfast?

Would you turn the clocks back and make your family late in the morning?

Would you dare to trick your teacher?

Do you feel happy when April Fools' Day is over?

Do you save your best tricks to fool your rival gang?

Do you enjoy making your best friend look a fool?

Just like Perfect Peter, you always get fooled – nah nah ne nah nah!

You love April Fools' Day and know lots of daring tricks, just like Horrid Henry. Nobody's safe when you're around!

Just like Moody Margaret, you're so mean and sneaky that you never get fooled! But your friends had better beware!

24

Moody Margaret's April Fools' Day Trick

READY SLICED BANANAS

You will need

A firm, ripe banana
A large, blunt-ended needle

Instructions

1. Carefully poke the needle through the banana skin close to the top.

2. Wiggle the needle from side to side inside the skin to cut a slice of banana.

3. Pull out the needle, then poke it into the skin again a bit further down and wiggle the needle to cut another slice.

4. Repeat this along the length of the banana, then put the banana back in the fruit bowl and wait for your victim.

5. The person who peels the banana will be surprised to find it's already sliced!

Easter Egg Games

Each player will need one hard boiled egg for all these games.

EGG TAPPING

Hold your egg in your hand, and tap it against the other player's egg.
The aim of the game is to break your friend's egg, without breaking your own. The winner plays the next person, until the overall winner is the last person left with an unbroken egg.

EGG ROLLING

Each player writes their name on their egg.
Next, stand at the top of a hill and roll your eggs down. The winner is the person whose egg rolls the furthest without breaking!

EGG HOPPING

In your garden, mark a start and a finish post. Each player lays their eggs on the ground somewhere between the two posts. Then take it in turns to hop from the start to the finish – without damaging any eggs. It's more difficult than you think!

Easter Egg Hunt

Count the times each character's face appears on an egg and write your answers in the spaces below.

Horrid Henry——— Perfect Peter——— Rabid Rebecca——— Stuck-up Steve —5— Mum —4—
Dad —2— Rude Ralph——— Grandma——— Soggy Sid———

Whose face is on the highest number of eggs? Whose face is on the lowest number of eggs?

_____   _____

27

Could You Survive Restaurant Le Posh?

1. Do you like bright, noisy restaurants with fast food? 5-10   YES/NO

2. Do you love burgers, chips and pizzas?   YES/NO

3. Do you hate trying new types of food?   YES/NO

4. Do you refuse to eat gloopy sauce?   YES/NO

5. Do you pick out all the green bits on your plate?   YES/NO

6. **Would you say 'Yuck' or 'Yum' if you were given:**

   (a) Tomatoes   5-10   YUCK/YUM

   (b) Squid   YUCK/YUM

   (c) Beetroot   YUCK/YUM

   (d) Spinach   YUCK/YUM

   (e) Sprouts   YUCK/YUM

   (f) Mussels   YUCK/YUM

   (g) Tripe   YUCK/YUM

   (h) Snails   YUCK/YUM

7. When you're having your dinner, do you?

(a) Put your elbows on the table   YES/NO

(b) Slouch   YES/NO

(c) Slurp   YES/NO

(d) Eat with your mouth wide open   YES/NO

(e) Kick your little brother and sister under the table   YES/NO

(f) Eat with your fingers   YES/NO

(g) Pull a face and say 'Yeeuch' when your food arrives   YES/NO

How many times did you circle YES and YUCK?

11–20: Rock stars love Restaurant Le Posh – but you'd hate it! It doesn't serve burgers, chips or pizzas and you have to eat things you've never heard of, all covered in sloppy, gloppy sauce. Gobble and Go's the place for you!

5–10: If you mind your manners and only slurp and slouch when no one's looking, you might just survive a meal at Restaurant Le Posh. Horrid Henry liked the food there because it was *so* revolting – give it a try and you might like it too!

1–4: You like funny, fancy food and your manners are perfect – you'll fit right in at Restaurant Le Posh. You might even be invited to join the top rock star table. But beware – if you can't read the French menu, you might end up with something you weren't expecting!

Horrid Henry Dines at Restaurant Le Posh

The restaurant was hushed. The tables were covered in snowy-white tablecloths, with yellow silk chairs. Huge gold chandeliers dangled from the ceiling. Crystal glasses twinkled. The rectangular china plates sparkled. Horrid Henry was impressed.

"Wow," said Henry. It was like walking into a palace.

"Haven't you ever been here before?" sneered Stuck-Up Steve.

"No," said Henry.

"*We* eat here all the time," said Steve. "I guess you're too poor."

"It's 'cause *we'd* rather eat at Whopper Whoopee," lied Henry.

"Hush, Steve," said Rich Aunt Ruby. "I'm sure Whopper Whoopee is a lovely restaurant." Steve snorted.

Henry kicked him under the table.

"OWWWW!" yelped Steve. "Henry kicked me!"

"No I didn't," said Henry. "It was an accident."

"Henry," said Mum through gritted teeth. "Remember what we said about best behaviour? We're in a fancy restaurant."

Horrid Henry scowled. He looked cautiously around. It was just as he'd feared. Everyone was busy eating weird bits of this and that, covered in gloopy sauces. Henry checked under the tables to see if anyone was being sick yet.

There was no one lying poisoned under the tables. I guess it's just a matter of time, thought Henry grimly. You won't catch me eating anything here.

Does Henry ever eat anything at Restaurant Le Posh? Find out in '**Horrid Henry Dines at Restaurant Le Posh**' in *Horrid Henry and the Mega-Mean Time Machine*.

Foul Foods

Yeuch! Can you find the foul foods in the criss-cross puzzle?

5 letters
LIVER
SQUID

6 letters
SNAILS

7 letters
SPINACH
OYSTERS
MUSSELS

8 letters
BEETROOT

11 letters
CAULIFLOWER

CLUE: FILL IN THE LONGEST WORD FIRST.

Do you know which of these foul foods Horrid Henry likes?

Foul foods

Horrid Henry's Rock Star Demands

Rock stars like me deserve the best of everything. I'm not waiting till my birthday. I'm not waiting till Christmas. In fact, I'm not waiting another minute! Mum! Dad! If I don't get everything I want, right now, I…I…I won't let you come to my concerts. So shape up!

1 The biggest bedroom in the house, with every wall covered in gigantic TVs. Mum and Dad can sleep in the kitchen. I need my old room for all my rock star costumes, and Peter's room for all my kit.

2 I always get to watch what I want to watch on TV – no one else can touch the TV remote.

3 Every Screamin' Demon and Mutant Max comic ever written to be delivered to me immediately.

4 A limousine available 24/7 with satellite TV and jacuzzi, and a spare one just in case.

5 Peter to be sent straight to prison for being the world's biggest toad.

6 My own gigantic fridge filled with Fizzywizz drinks and Chunky Chocolate Fab Fudge Caramel Delight ice cream.

7 Moody Margaret to fetch me all the burgers and chips I can eat from Gobble and Go.

8 Only ever have pizza, chips, crisps and burgers for dinner.

9 My very own comfy black chair, only and exclusively for me.

33

Rock Bands Double Puzzle

Untangle the words and fit them into the
spaces to complete the names of the bands.

ESLYML   **YFDFA**
TSRA   **RRLLIED**
LKSUL   **URDM**
YRIAH

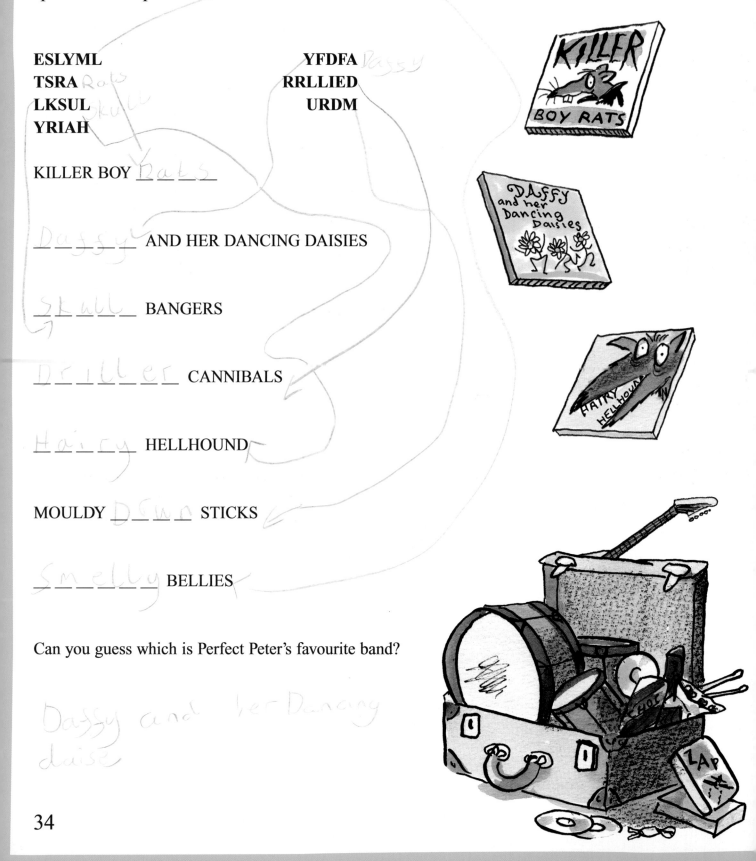

KILLER BOY _Rats_

Daffy AND HER DANCING DAISIES

Skull BANGERS

Driller CANNIBALS

Hairy HELLHOUND

MOULDY _Drum_ STICKS

Smelly BELLIES

Can you guess which is Perfect Peter's favourite band?

Daffy and her Dancing
daise

34

Fit these rock band words into the criss-cross puzzle.

4 letters
RATS

5 letters
HAIRY
DAFFY

6 letters
MOULDY
KILLER
STICKS

7 letters
BELLIES
DAISIES
BANGERS

9 letters
CANNIBALS

CLUE:
FILL IN
THE LONGEST
WORD FIRST.

Aerobic Al's 2012 Games

Aerobic Al has come up with some Olympic games of his own – try them with your friends!

TOSSING THE WELLY

1. Mark a starting line with string or chalk.
2. Each player runs up to the starting line and tosses their welly as far as they can, while their supporters shout, "Give it some welly!"
3. The person who throws their welly the furthest is the winner.

AEROBIC AL'S RULES

- Always play this game outside where there's plenty of space.
- If you cross the starting line, your throw won't count.

PAPER PLANES

1. All players make their own paper planes, with their name or initials written on.
2. Mark a starting line with string or chalk.
3. Each player flies their plane from the starting line, and the person whose plane flies the furthest is the winner.

AEROBIC AL'S RULES

- The distance the plane flies is measured straight ahead from the starting line to the place where the plane lands.
- It's good luck if the wind blows your plane in the right direction and bad luck if it doesn't!

FIRING BALLOON ROCKETS

You will need

Sausage-shaped balloons
Chairs
String
Straws
Sticky tape
Paperclips

1. Cut a piece of string three metres long and thread it through a straw.
2. Tie one end of the string to a chair, then tie the other end to another chair and move the chairs apart so the string is pulled tight.
3. Blow up a balloon and put a paperclip on the end to stop the air escaping, then tape the balloon to the straw lengthways.
4. Push the straw and the balloon to one end of the string, with the end facing the chair.
6. Take off the paperclip and release the balloon. Watch it whiz from one end of the string to the other!
7. Each player needs to set up their own string, straw, balloon and chairs. Then all the players set them off at the same time, and the first balloon to reach the other end of the string is the winner!

AEROBICS AL'S TOP TIP
• The bigger you blow up your balloon, the faster it'll go!

Perfect Peter's Pencil and Paper Page

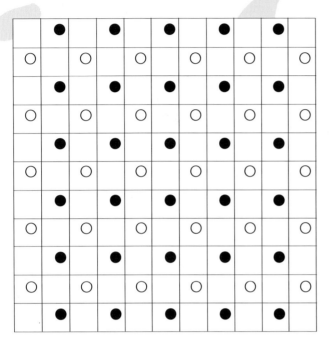

One player has a **RED** pen. He draws from top to bottom, joining up the **BLACK** dots.

One player has a **BLUE** pen. He draws from left to right, joining up the **WHITE** dots.

How to play

1. Copy the grid of dots above, with both black and white dots.
2. Starting anywhere, the player with the red pen goes first, and joins up two black dots. The player with the blue pen joins up two white dots.
3. The aim of the game is to be the first player to connect one side of the grid to the other.
4. The players can only join dots of their own colour and can only join dots that are next to each other across or down.
5. None of the lines can cross.

In this game, both players have had 2 turns.

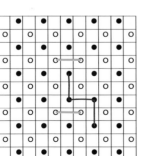

This game is finished, and the blue player is the winner.

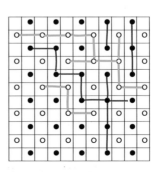

38

Greedy Graham's Grub

MELTED MARSHMALLOWS

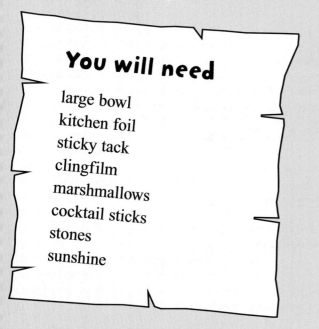

You will need

large bowl
kitchen foil
sticky tack
clingfilm
marshmallows
cocktail sticks
stones
sunshine

Instructions

1. Line the bowl with foil. Press a piece of sticky tack down in the middle of the bowl.

2. Put a marshmallow on the end of a cocktail stick, then push the other end of the cocktail stick into the sticky tack.

3. Cover the top of the bowl with clingfilm, then put the bowl outside in a sunny place.

4. Position the bowl so that the inside is facing the sun.

5. Leave for about 15 minutes.

6. If the marshmallow gets hot enough, it'll start to melt. If it doesn't, leave it for another 15 minutes.

7. Enjoy your gooey melted marshmallow. Mmmm!

Henry's Holiday Money-Making Tips

SET UP A STALL TO SELL ALL THE STUFF YOU DON'T WANT

- Even if you hate all your clothes, books and unwanted presents – somebody else will be silly enough to pay good money for them, tee hee!
- Mums and dads have lots of useless things they don't need – just take a look around the house.
- Always run the stall by yourself – then you won't have to share your earnings.
- You can get a great price for your little brothers or sisters if you sell them as slaves.

GO BUSKING

- If you're a brilliant rock star like me, why not go busking?
- Make a big sign, saying: GIVE GENEROUSLY.
- Sing as loudly as you can – the louder the better!
- Tell people they're lucky to get this amazing chance to hear you singing in the street – so they'd better pay up!

40

MARVELLOUS MAKEOVERS

- You can make loads of money just by smearing coloured gunk onto people's faces.
- Charge everyone a lot of money – then they'll know that you're a proper makeover expert.
- Tell your family and friends that they're ugly warty old toads – then they'll be desperate for an expensive makeover!

- Don't let anyone see what you're doing until you've completely finished. Then say, "You look amazing!" If you say it loudly enough, they'll believe you.

- Refuse to give anyone their money back, even if they think they look horrible.

Killer Boy Rats Rock Lyrics

Here are some amazing lyrics sent in by runners-up in the lyrics competition. But who will be the Christmas Number One? Stay tuned to find out!

We're the Killer Boy Rats and we've Come to Say
We Bash and we Crash Every Single Day!
We're Loud and Proud and we're Rough and Tough
You Don't Wanna get in a Fight With Us!

Cuz You Know
THAT WE'RE THE KILLER BOY RATS

Evan, 7

I'm in school,
And I'm getting bored.
The school bell rings,
And I start to sing!

Don't wanna be a goodie goodie goodie,
I wanna wear a Parka or a Hoodie,
Don't wanna be a goodie goodie goodie in school.

Robert, 10

Purple Hand Gang rocks,
we are so cool,
watch out for us,
coolest in school.

I don't wanna be bossed around,
by teachers, mums or dads, dogs or cats,
Cos I'm just being horrid,
I'm one of the Killer Boy Rats

Don't tell me what to do,
or how to be me,
cos when I'm king I'll show you all,
Just you wait and see!

Pip, 7

Who's Your Favourite Band?

1. **How loud do you like your music?**
   (a) As loud as a rock concert ✓
   (b) Loud enough to fill the school hall
   (c) Just loud enough to hear, but not
       loud enough to disturb Mum and Dad

2. **Which best describes your dancing style?**
   (a) Stomping and stamping ✓
   (b) Shuffling and clapping
   (c) Hopping and skipping

3. **Do you like to sing along with your favourite music?**
   (a) No – I like to shout and scream! ✓
   (b) If everyone else is singing, I'll sing too
   (c) Yes, a sing-a-long is such fun, tra la la la la

4. **What would be a good logo for your favourite band?**
   (a) Skull and crossbones ✓
   (b) School tie
   (c) A circle of pretty flowers

5. **At your band's concert, there's a special guest star. Is it…**
   (a) Mad Moon Madison on drums? ✓
   (b) Miss Battle-Axe on the tambourine?
   (c) Busy Lizzie singing and dancing?

44

6. **Which of these do you think are the best lyrics?**
    (a) I'm in my coffin, no time for coughin' ✓
    (b) One day my prince will come
    (c) Tippy-toe daisy do, let us sing a song for you

7. **If you had a favourite album,**
   would it be called?
    (a) Splat! ✓
    (b) School of Rock
    (c) Whoops-a-Daisy and other Super Songs

8. **What's your favourite type of music?**
    (a) Rock ✓
    (b) A mixture of styles
    (c) Pop

Mostly (a)s:
Just like Horrid Henry, you like your bands loud and rockin'!
If you drive your parents mad by shouting and stomping along to your
favourite music and making your house shake, you'd love one of Henry's
favourites like the Killer Boy Rats, the Skullbangers or the Smelly Bellies.

Mostly (b)s:
It sounds like Horrid Henry's School Rock Band is your type of music!
Turn to page 62 to find out who joins in when Henry entertains the school at Christmas.

Mostly (c)s:
You'd love to join Perfect Peter and sing along sweetly
with Daffy and her Dancing Daisies. So much nicer than
the horrible loud noise that Horrid Henry likes.

Horrid Henry's Timetable

It's time for Horrid Henry to go back to school and his parents have stuck up a timetable to help him organise his week.

MONDAY	TUESDAY	WEDNESDAY	THURSDAY
REMEMBER PENCIL CASE, SCHOOL BOOKS AND <u>HEALTHY</u> PACKED LUNCH I don't want a healthy lunch – I want crisps, biscuits and chocolate!	DON'T FORGET – PE KIT AND PACKED LUNCH. I'm sick, I need a note.	PACKED LUNCH One grape is enough. I want sweets! LUNCHTIME STAMP CLUB I'm not going to stupid stamp club! ROCK STARS DON'T COLLECT STAMPS!	SWIMMING – TAKE TOWEL, TRUNKS AND PACKED LUNCH. Horrible, the worst day of the week.

But Henry doesn't want to go back to school – he's a wild and crazy rock star and he'll do what he wants, *when* he wants!

FRIDAY	SATURDAY	SUNDAY
PACKED LUNCH	Sleeping in	
	DANCE CLASS AT MISS TUTU'S For peter	FAMILY WALK for Mum, Dad and Peter. Henry can stay at home.
I'll swap with Greedy Graham, ha ha!	**Peter's chores** HOOVERING TIDY BEDROOM	No school No Miss Battle-Axe Loud music all day!
~~CHOIR~~ ROCK BAND PRACTICE	Morning TV Afternoon TV Evening TV	

Could You Be Chosen to Meet the Queen?

1. How would you describe yourself?
- (a) Polite and perfect
- (b) Nice and friendly
- (c) Loud and rude ✓

2. Why do you think you should be chosen to meet the Queen?
- (a) I'm always very good at school
- (b) I'd really like to meet her
- (c) I want to ask her how many TVs she has ✓

3. Do you have any special skills?
- (a) I have perfect manners
- (b) I play the recorder
- (c) I can eat a bag of crisps in record time ✓

4. What would you wear to meet the Queen?
- (a) Your best party clothes
- (b) Your school uniform – even if it's a bit dirty
- (c) Jeans and a tee shirt ✓

5. Which do you think is the best order for your presentation?

(a) Bow, present the bouquet, answer the Queen's question, walk away

(b) Bow, walk away, walk back, present the bouquet

(c) Bow, stick out your tongue, push the bouquet in her face ✓

6. How many times would you practise your presentation?

(a) As many times as I can – I want to be perfect on the day

(a) About 5 times should be enough

(b) I don't need to practise – it's easy-peasy! ✓

7. What's the first thing you'd say to the Queen?

(a) Your Majesty

(b) Please don't chop off my head

(c) How many TVs do you have? ✓

8. How would you feel if you were the one chosen to meet the Queen?

(a) Honoured

(b) Thrilled

(c) The best boy/girl won! ✓

Count how many (a)s, (b)s and (c)s you have.

Mostly (a)s: With your lovely manners and smart clothes, you'll be the ideal choice to meet the Queen. Enjoy your big day!

Mostly (b)s: You're not quite up the top task of presenting flowers to the Queen, but you're so enthusiastic you deserve to be on the front row or chosen to entertain her on your recorder.

Mostly (c)s: Just like Horrid Henry, you'd be the worst choice to meet the Queen. You need to be kept as far away from her as possible. If you're off sick the day the Queen comes to visit, your teacher will be very happy!

Horrid Henry Meets the Queen

Perfect Peter bowed to himself in the mirror.

"Your Majesty," he said, pretending to present a bouquet. "Welcome to our school, Your Majesty. My name is Peter, Your Majesty. Thank you, Your Majesty. Goodbye, Your Majesty." Slowly Perfect Peter retreated backwards, bowing and smiling.

"Oh shut up," snarled Horrid Henry. He glared at Peter. If Peter said "Your Majesty" one more time, he would, he would – Horrid Henry wasn't sure what he'd do, but it would be horrible.

The Queen was coming to Henry's school! The real live Queen! The real live Queen, with her dogs and jewels and crowns and castles and beefeaters and knights and horses and ladies-in-waiting, was coming to see the Tudor wall they had built.

Yet for some reason Horrid Henry had not been asked to give the Queen a bouquet. Instead, the head, Mrs Oddbod, had chosen Peter.

Peter!

Why stupid smelly old ugly toad Peter? It was so unfair. Just because Peter had more stars than anyone in the 'Good as Gold' book, was that any reason to choose *him*? Henry should have been chosen. He would do a much better job than Peter. Besides, he wanted to ask the Queen how many TVs she had. Now he'd never get the chance.

"Your Majesty," said Peter, bowing.

"Your Majesty," mimicked Henry, curtseying.

Perfect Peter ignored him. He'd been ignoring Henry a lot ever since *he'd* been chosen to meet the Queen. Come to think of it, everyone had been ignoring Henry.

"Isn't it thrilling?" said Mum for the millionth time.

"Isn't it fantastic?" said Dad for the billionth time.

"NO!" Henry had said. Who'd want to hand some rotten flowers to a stupid queen, anyhow? Not Horrid Henry. And he certainly didn't want to have his picture in the paper, and everyone making a fuss.

"Bow, bouquet, answer her question, walk away," muttered Perfect Peter. Then he paused. "Or is it bouquet, bow?"

Horrid Henry had had just about enough of Peter showing off.

"You're doing it all wrong," said Henry.

"No, I'm not," said Peter.

"Yes you are," said Henry. "You're supposed to hold the bouquet up to her nose, so she can have a sniff before you give it to her."

Perfect Peter paused.

"No I'm not," said Peter.

Horrid Henry shook his head sadly. "I think we'd better practise," he said. "Pretend I'm the Queen." He picked up Peter's shiny silver crown, covered in fool's jewels, and put it on his head.

Perfect Peter beamed. He'd been begging Henry to practise with him all morning.

Does Peter do it right on his big day? Does Henry ask the Queen how many TVs she has? Find out in **Horrid Henry Meets the Queen**.

What's Your Perfect Pet?

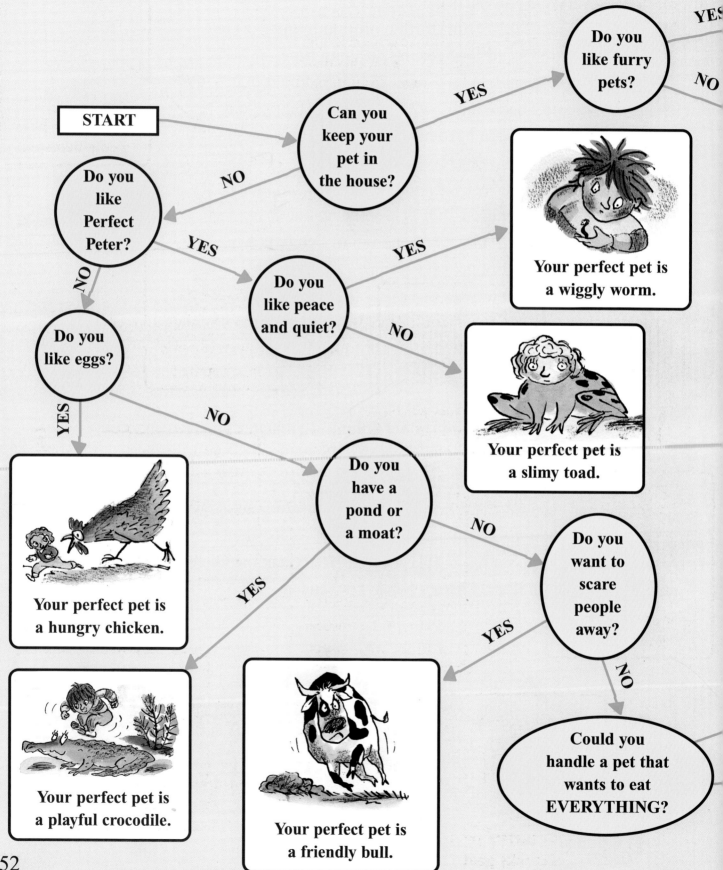

START

Can you keep your pet in the house?

YES Do you like furry pets?

YES

NO

NO Do you like Perfect Peter?

YES Do you like peace and quiet?

YES Your perfect pet is a wiggly worm.

NO Do you like eggs?

NO Your perfect pet is a slimy toad.

YES Your perfect pet is a hungry chicken.

NO Do you have a pond or a moat?

NO Do you want to scare people away?

YES Your perfect pet is a playful crocodile.

YES Your perfect pet is a friendly bull.

NO Could you handle a pet that wants to eat EVERYTHING?

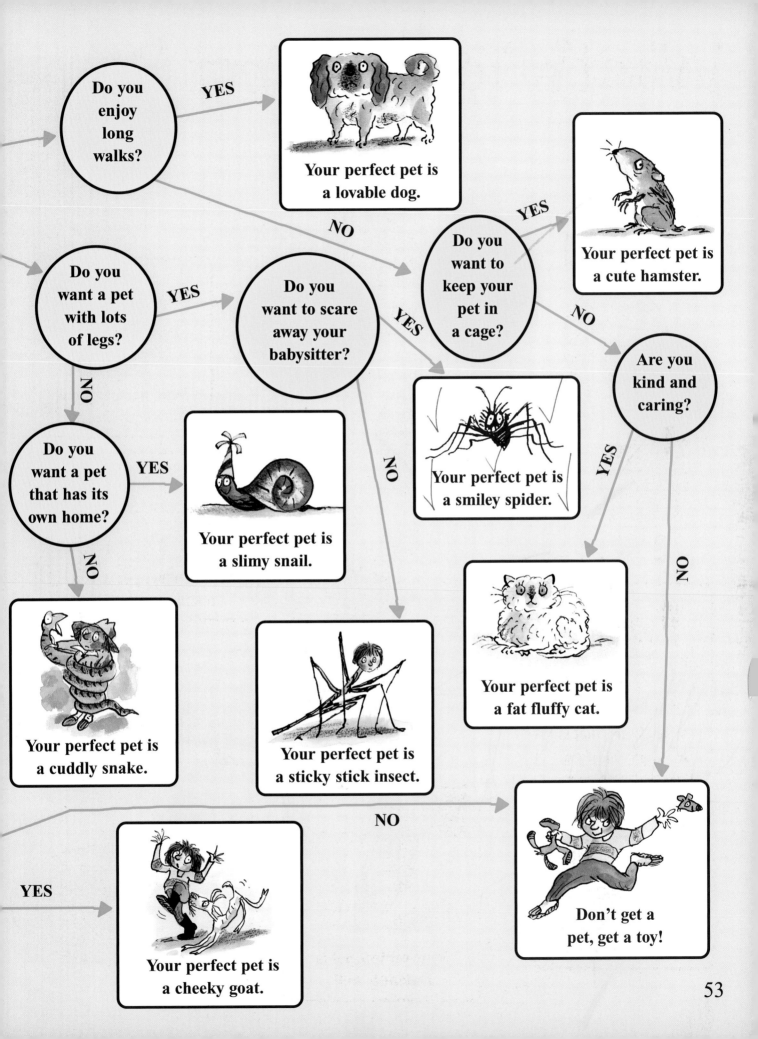

Do you enjoy long walks?

YES → Your perfect pet is a lovable dog.

NO →

Do you want a pet with lots of legs?

YES → **Do you want to scare away your babysitter?**

NO →

Do you want a pet that has its own home?

YES → Your perfect pet is a slimy snail.

NO → Your perfect pet is a cuddly snake.

YES → Your perfect pet is a cheeky goat.

Do you want to scare away your babysitter?

YES → Your perfect pet is a smiley spider.

NO → Your perfect pet is a sticky stick insect.

Do you want to keep your pet in a cage?

YES → Your perfect pet is a cute hamster.

NO → **Are you kind and caring?**

Are you kind and caring?

YES → Your perfect pet is a fat fluffy cat.

NO → Don't get a pet, get a toy!

53

Horrid Henry's Homework

Horrid Henry doesn't have time for homework. He has his glittering rock star future to plan. When Miss Battle-Axe asks the class to produce a family tree, this is what Henry hands in. One of these relatives isn't real – can you guess which one?

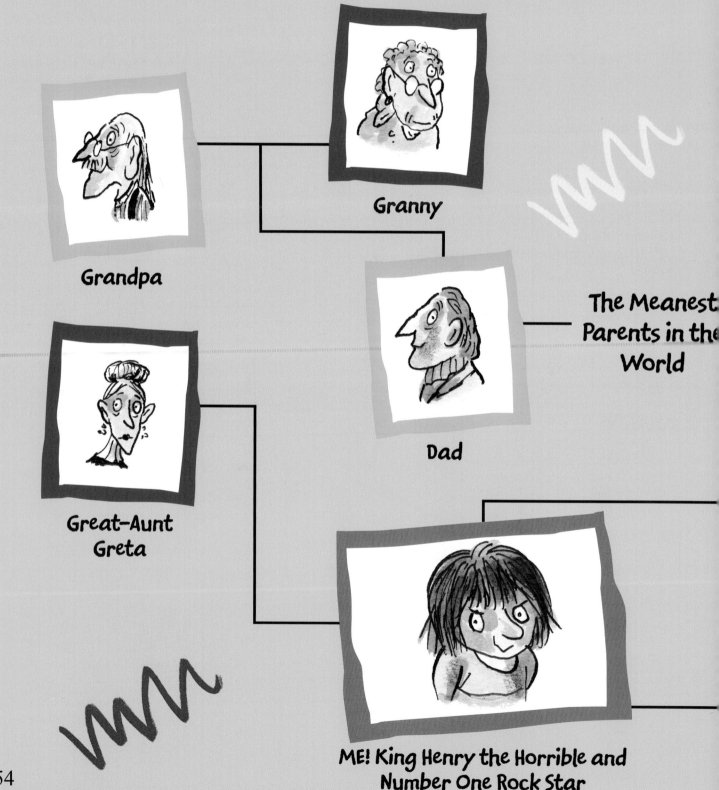

Granny

Grandpa

The Meanest Parents in the World

Dad

Great-Aunt Greta

ME! King Henry the Horrible and Number One Rock Star

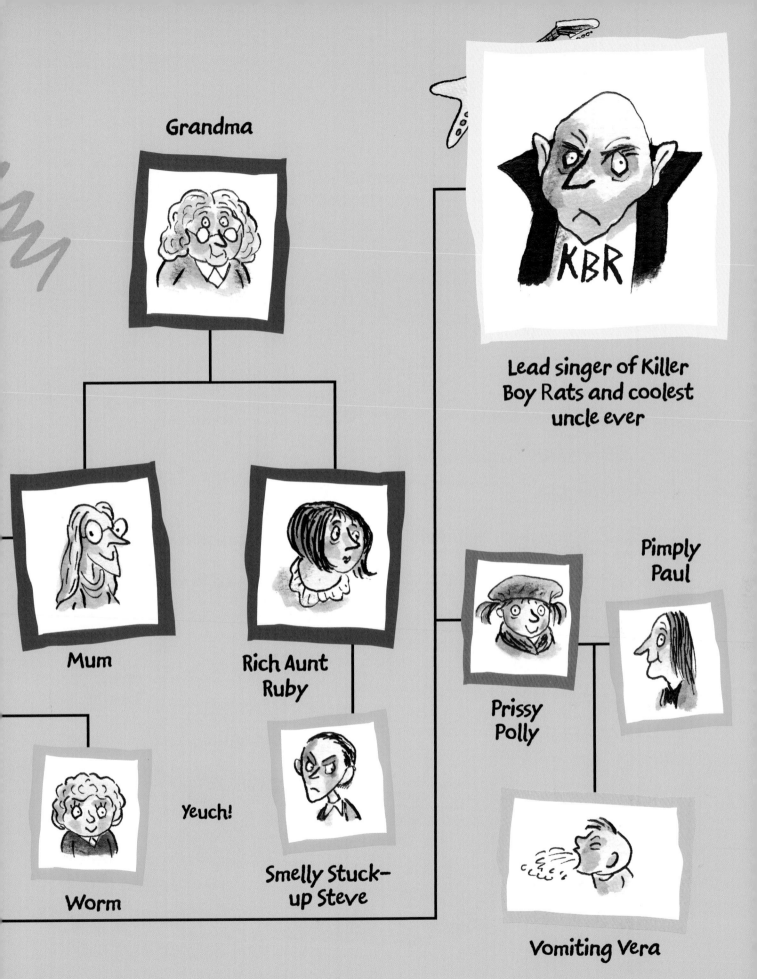

Grandma

Lead singer of Killer
Boy Rats and coolest
uncle ever

KBR

Mum

Rich Aunt
Ruby

Pimply
Paul

Prissy
Polly

Worm

Yeuch!

Smelly Stuck-
up Steve

Vomiting Vera

Show and Tell

At school, everyone brings one of their favourite belongings in for Show and Tell. Can you guess who brought what?

1. Horrid Henry   H
2. Moody Margaret   F
3. Aerobic Al   K
4. Brainy Brian   L
5. Greedy Graham   J
6. Jolly Josh   A
7. Gorgeous Gurinder   E
8. Rude Ralph   G
9. Weepy William   C
10. Lazy Linda   B
11. Kung-Fu Kate   I
12. Beefy Bert   D

A. joke book
B. sleeping bag
C. box of tissues
D. nothing – he forgot
E. mirror
F. pirate hat
G. whoopee cushion
H. Killer Boy Rats poster
I. black belt
J. cookbook
K. trainers
L. encyclopaedia

Spooky Spot the Difference

Can you spot the six differences?

1. _tooth / black_ 4. _dog missing ear_

2. _spike missing_ 5. _dog red teeth_

3. _lipstick/colour_ 6. _helmet studs_

Horrid Henry's Hallowe'en Top Tips

Horrid Henry loves Hallowe'en! A day when you're *supposed* to stuff your face with sweets and play horrid tricks. Here are his top tips for the perfect trick or treat experience.

TRICK -OR-TREAT CHECKLIST

Most important of all is a HUGE bag to collect all your treats ✔

A brilliant scary costume (see right) ✔

A great bag of tricks ✔

MAKE SURE YOU GET PROPER TREATS

Chocolate Hairballs ✔

Belcher Squelchers ✔

Spiky Spiders ✔

apples ✗

satsumas ✗

walnuts ✗

Wear a Cool and Scary costume

Red-and-black devil ✔ ✓

Mummy ✔ ✓

Vampire ✔ ✓

Zombie ✔ ✓

Pink polka dot bunny ✘ ✗ (definitely!)

Practise an Evil Laugh— heh heh heh!

DON'T take your little brother or sister - especially if they look really stupid. If they really, really have to go with you, lend them a costume.

Perfect Peter's TOP TIP
- Smile sweetly
- Be polite and not too scary

59

More Killer Boy Rats Rock Lyrics

It's nearly time to announce the Christmas Number One. But first, here are some more rocking runners-up…

oh kids just rule

parents don't know that that's why they're so cruel

you can never be sure

when a parent opens your door

when you're stuck in your room

sing a little tune say

you will never catch me

I will snatch the key to open my door

you will never catch me

because kids rule!

Pari, 10

we are the Killer Boy Rats!
oh yeaaaah
we are the Killer Boy Rats!
that's right
we like to stomp to the beat!
and try to eat everything that squeaks!
we love to rock and roll all round!
I'm fighting a mummy!
don't need my mummy!
we are the Killer Boy Rats!
ohh yeaah!

Hassan, 11

School Christmas Concert Crossword

Horrid Henry and his classmates put together a band to entertain the school at the Christmas concert. Can you answer the clues from the pictures below and fill in the crossword?

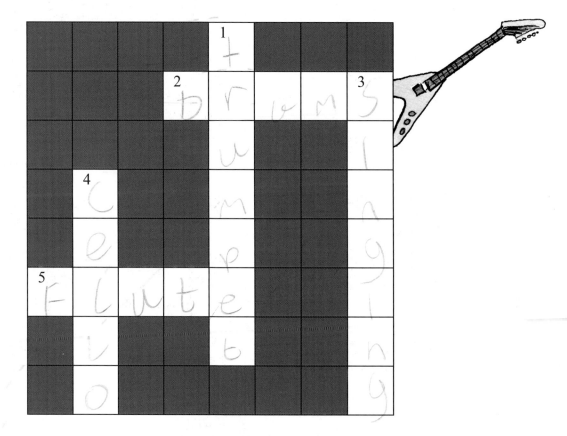

CLUES

Down

1. What brass instrument is Moody Margaret playing?
3. What is Soraya doing?
4. Perfect Peter is playing which string instrument?

Across

2. What is Horrid Henry playing?
5. What woodwind instrument is Weepy William playing?

Rock Roles

Horrid Henry wants to be the lead singer, the drummer *and* the manager of a rock band. What's your ideal role?

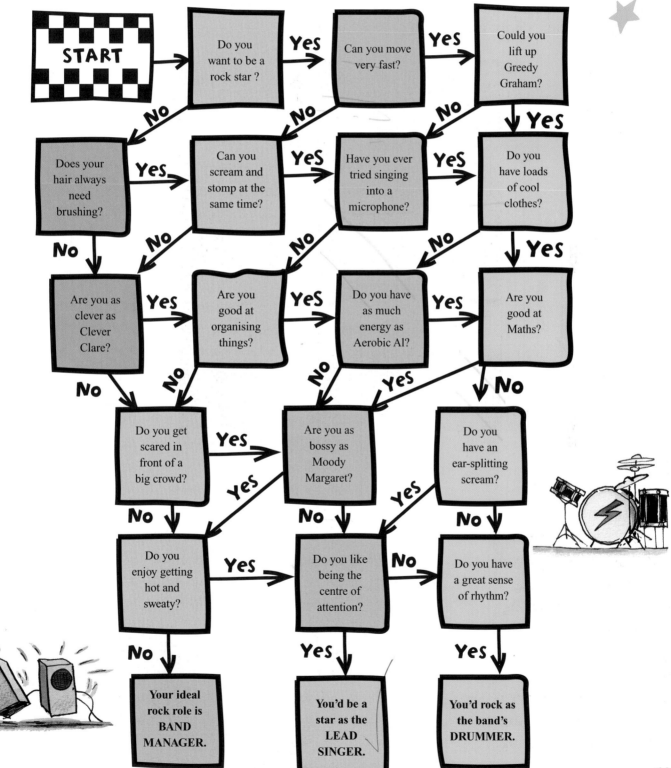

START

Do you want to be a rock star? — **Yes** → Can you move very fast? — **Yes** → Could you lift up Greedy Graham? — **Yes**

Do you want to be a rock star? — **No**

Can you move very fast? — **No**

Could you lift up Greedy Graham? — **Yes**

Does your hair always need brushing? — **Yes** → Can you scream and stomp at the same time? — **Yes** → Have you ever tried singing into a microphone? — **Yes** → Do you have loads of cool clothes?

Have you ever tried singing into a microphone? — **Yes** → Do you have loads of cool clothes?

Can you scream and stomp at the same time? — **No**

Have you ever tried singing into a microphone? — **No**

Does your hair always need brushing? — **No**

Do you have loads of cool clothes? — **Yes**

Are you as clever as Clever Clare? — **Yes** → Are you good at organising things? — **Yes** → Do you have as much energy as Aerobic Al? — **Yes** → Are you good at Maths?

Are you good at organising things? — **No**

Do you have as much energy as Aerobic Al? — **No**

Are you as clever as Clever Clare? — **No**

Do you have as much energy as Aerobic Al? — **Yes**

Are you good at Maths? — **No**

Do you get scared in front of a big crowd? — **Yes** → Are you as bossy as Moody Margaret?

Do you get scared in front of a big crowd? — **No**

Are you as bossy as Moody Margaret? — **No**

Do you have an ear-splitting scream? — **No**

Do you enjoy getting hot and sweaty? — **Yes** → Do you like being the centre of attention? — **No** → Do you have a great sense of rhythm?

Are you as bossy as Moody Margaret? — **Yes** → Do you have a great sense of rhythm?

Do you enjoy getting hot and sweaty? — **No** → **Your ideal rock role is BAND MANAGER.**

Do you like being the centre of attention? — **Yes** → **You'd be a star as the LEAD SINGER.**

Do you have a great sense of rhythm? — **Yes** → **You'd rock as the band's DRUMMER.**

63

Horrid Henry's Rock Star Christmas List

Horrid Henry wants the best Christmas presents EVER this year. Find the items from his present list in the word search. The remaining letters spell out what his mum really buys him.

TELEVISION
CASTLE
MOTORBIKE
SNAKE
GUITAR

DRUMKIT
SPEEDBOAT
HELICOPTER
COMPUTER

S	P	E	E	D	B	O	A	T	N
C	J	R	K	I	G	S	A	O	M
A	W	A	A	P	U	Z	I	O	Z
S	L	T	N	E	V	S	T	E	S
T	T	I	S	S	I	O	A	N	D
L	H	U	A	V	R	N	D	K	E
E	R	G	E	B	C	H	I	E	F
H	E	L	I	C	O	P	T	E	R
S	E	K	T	I	K	M	U	R	D
T	E	C	O	M	P	U	T	E	R

What does Mum really buy for Henry?

Jigsaw puzzle, vests and
handkerchiefs

64

Moody Margaret's No-Currants Christmas Cake

Horrid Henry and Moody Margaret agree on one thing – currants, raisins and sultanas are HORRIBLE! They don't like mince pies, Christmas pudding or Christmas cake. Here's Moody Margaret's Christmas cake with no currants and lots of chocolate.

You will need

1 tbsp sugar
1 tbsp golden syrup
85g butter or margarine
2 tbsp cocoa
225g digestive biscuits
225g chocolate
20cm square baking tin

Instructions

1. Grease your tin with butter.
2. Put biscuits inside a plastic bag and crush them with a rolling pin.
3. Put the sugar, golden syrup and butter in a pan and ask an adult to help you melt them over a low heat.
4. Remove the pan from the heat and stir in the crushed biscuits.
5. Put the mixture into your baking tin and press down with a spoon.
6. Leave to cool in the fridge.
7. Ask an adult to help you melt the chocolate in a bowl over a pan of gently steaming water, then spread all over your biscuit cake.
8. When the chocolate has set, cut it into big pieces and enjoy!

Horrid Henry Minds His Manners

Horrid Henry snatched his letter and tore open the green envelope. The foul stink of mouldy socks wafted out.

> Yo Henry!
> Marvin the Maniac here. You sound just like the kind of crazy guy we want on Gross-Out! Be at TV Centre next Saturday at 9.00 a.m. and gross us out! It's a live broadcast, so anything can happen!
> Marvin

"I've been invited to be a contestant on *Gross-Out*!" screamed Henry, dancing up and down the stairs. It was a dream come true. "I'll be shooting it out with Tank Thomas and Tapioca Tina while eating as much ice cream as I can!"

"Absolutely not!" said Mum. "You will not go on that disgusting show!"

"Agreed," said Dad. "That show is revolting."

"It's meant to be revolting!" said Horrid Henry. "That's the point."

"N-O spells no," said Mum.

"You're the meanest, most horrible parents in the whole world," screamed Henry. "I hate you!" He threw himself on the sofa and wailed. "I WANT TO BE ON *GROSS-OUT*! I WANT TO BE ON *GROSS-OUT*!"

Does Henry meet Marvin the Maniac at TV Centre? Find out in '**Horrid Henry Minds His Manners**' in **Horrid Henry's Haunted House**.

Meet Marvin the Maniac

Help Horrid Henry find his way along the corridors of TV Centre to meet Marvin the Maniac in the *Gross-Out* studio.

START
▼

Which TV Show?

It's your big chance to star in one of TV's top Christmas Special Shows.
But which is the best show for you?

Tick to answer YES or NO	YES	NO
1. Do you enjoy watching the same programmes as your little brother or sister?		✓
2. Do you love pretty flowers?		✓
3. Would you like to dress up as a flower?		✓
4. Are you a good dancer?		✓
5. Do you enjoy sing-alongs?		✓

If you ticked more YES's, you'd make a delightful dancing prancing daisy in DAFFY AND HER DANCING DAISIES.
If you ticked more NOs, go to question 6.

	YES	NO
6. Do you always say "please" and "thank you"?		✓
7. Would you rather eat with a knife and fork than with your fingers?		✓
8. Do you think eating with your mouth open is rude?		✓
9. Do you always remember to write your thank-you letters?		✓
10. Can you eat soup without slurping?		

**If you ticked more YES's, you'd be the perfect guest in …
MANNERS WITH MAGGIE.**
If you ticked more NOs, go to question 11.

Tick to answer YES or NO	YES	NO
11. Are you very lazy?	✓	
12. Do you like sleeping late into the afternoon?	✓	
13. Are your parents always telling you that your bedroom is a pigsty?		✓
14. Would you feel proud if your bedroom was the most disgusting ever seen?	✓	
15. Do you think Dirty Dirk is a great name for a TV show host?	✓	

If you ticked more YES's, you should join in… HOG HOUSE, where children compete to see whose room is the most disgusting.

If you ticked more NOs, go to question 16.

	YES	NO
16. Do you have a special talent that you'd like to show off on TV?	✓	
17. Do you think it would be more fun to sing and dance on TV than to blast someone with goo?		✓
18. Would you like to become famous?	✓	
19. Do you find it hard to eat lots and lots of ice cream?		
20. Would you be upset if you got covered in goo?	✓	✓

If you ticked more YES's, you should take a star turn in TALENT TIGERS…

If you ticked more NOs, you'd enjoy the goo-shooting, food-gobbling extravanganza GROSS-OUT!

The Killer Boy Rats' Christmas Number One

And now, the moment we've all been waiting for – the Christmas Number One. The winner of the Killer Boy Rats lyrics competition is…

Rats, rats we want to rock
with the rats,
When rats come knocking the crowd
will be rocking
Get off your bums and play
those drums

Let's go far and play that guitar
Like you have never seen before
Let's all get on the dance floor.
Rock with the rats!

Merridy, 10

Christmas Rock Star

Instead of a boring old star at the top of your Christmas tree, make your own special rock star!

You will need

Scissors
Stiff card – gold or red is best for Christmas
Hole punch
Ribbon or string
Glue
A picture of your favourite rock star

Instructions

1. Using the star template, cut out a card star.
2. Punch a hole in the top and thread a piece of ribbon through to hang it from the tree.
3. Glue your rock star in the centre of the star.

Puzzle Answers

Page 11

There are **9** rock guitars hidden in the Annual.

Page 17

New Year's Eve Word Search

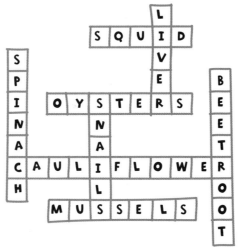

Page 18-19

Brainy Brian's Noisy New Year Quiz

1. (a)
2. (b)
3. (c)
4. (a)
5. (b)
6. (a)
7. (c)
8. (b)

Page 23

Pancake Day Puzzle

	NUMBER OF PANCAKES	FAVOURITE FILLING
HORRID HENRY	5	Chocolate sauce
PERFECT PETER	2	Lemon juice
GREEDY GRAHAM	8	Jam

Page 27

Easter Egg Hunt

Rude Ralph's face is on the highest number of eggs (5)

Grandma's face is on the lowest number of eggs (3)

There are 4 of all the other faces.

Page 31

Foul Foods

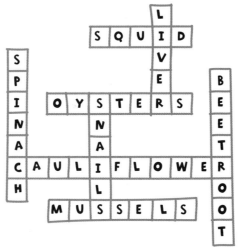

Page 34

Rock Bands Double Puzzle

KILLER BOY **RATS**

DAFFY AND HER DANCING DAISIES

SKULLBANGERS

DRILLER CANNIBALS

HAIRY HELLHOUND

MOULDY **DRUM**STICKS

SMELLY BELLIES

Page 35

Rock Bands Double Puzzle

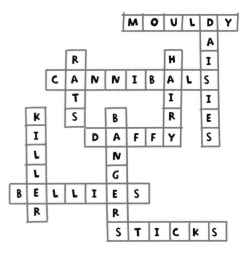

Page 56
Show and Tell

1 – H
2 – F
3 – K
4 – L
5 – J
6 – A
7 – E
8 – G
9 – C
10 – B
11 – I
12 – D

Page 57
Spooky Spot the Difference

1. One of the man's teeth is black.
2. One of the spikes from the lady's necklace is missing.
3. The lady's lipstick is a different colour.
4. One of the dogs is missing an ear.
5. One of the dogs has red teeth.
6. The lady's helmet has more studs.

Page 62
School Christmas Concert Crossword

Page 67
Meet Marvin the Maniac

Page 64
Horrid Henry's Rock Star Christmas List

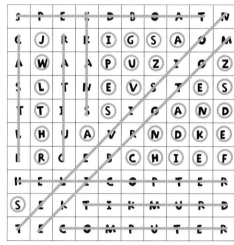

Henry's mum buys him
JIGSAW PUZZLE, VESTS
AND HANDKERCHIEFS

You can read these other *Horrid Henry* titles, stories available as audio editions, read by Miranda Richardson